jewelry crafting
with kids

jewelry crafting
with kids

35 creative jewelry projects
for children to make and wear

sarah fiorenza
photography by **penny wincer**

RYLAND
PETERS
& SMALL

LONDON NEW YORK

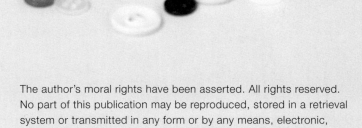

Senior Designers Barbara Zuñiga & Sonya Nathoo
Editor Rebecca Woods
Location Research Emily Westlake
Production Laura Grundy
Art Director Leslie Harrington
Editorial Director Julia Charles

Stylist Luis Peral
Indexer Hilary Bird

First published in 2012
by **Ryland Peters & Small**
20–21 Jockey's Fields
London WC1R 4BW
and
519 Broadway, 5th Floor
New York, NY 10012

www.rylandpeters.com

10 9 8 7 6 5 4 3 2 1

Text © Sarah Fiorenza 2012

Design and photographs
© Ryland Peters & Small 2012

ISBN 978 1 84975 214 5

A catalogue record for this book is available from
the British Library.

US Library of Congress cataloging-in-publication data
has been applied for.

Printed in China

contents

introduction

As a little girl, the biggest excitement for me when going to my grandma's house was to be allowed to rummage through a small box of assorted buttons and jewellery. My grandma was a keen crafter and loved to do a variety of things, from hand-painting ceramics to making cloth toys for all the grandchildren. I have been hugely influenced by both her and my mum, who is also brilliant at sewing and crafting.

I am a firm believer that the things you enjoy doing as a child serve as a barometer of what you'll enjoy as an adult, and encouraging children to bring out their creative side is extremely rewarding for them and may even lay the foundation for a future passion. During the making of this book my daughter Annaliese, aged five, really loved getting involved with the projects and is already a keen collector of ribbon and gift wrap. And my son Giuseppe, aged two, also really enjoyed taking his time to thread wooden beads onto cord.

For children today everything moves at such a fast pace and so sitting down and taking the time to make something with their own hands can give a real sense of achievement. Jewellery making is perfect for kids. It's small scale is great for little hands to work on, and being able to wear and show off what they have made gives an extra level of enjoyment.

This creative book includes 35 projects for you to make with your children, or for older children to tackle alone. There is something for kids of all ages and all abilities, from pom pom necklaces made with wool to animal brooches made from gift wrap and card. The projects vary in difficulty, ranging from very simple beading projects to more complicated techniques involving sewing and modelling with colourful clay. Nearly all the projects can be made easily and without using specific tools. And as each project is broken down into simple-to-follow steps, they are all easy to make.

With jewellery making there are no hard and fast rules for the materials you can use. The projects in this book are based on a variety of simple materials such as buttons, felt, wire and paper, which are readily available from good craft suppliers and the high street. But beyond that, you can put to use whatever there is to hand and whatever brings inspiration. Jewellery making really brings out the collector in kids, so encourage them to keep any little objects that they find, like shells or buttons and ribbon as they may be able to incorporate them into a necklace, bracelet, brooch or hair adornment. Little scraps of fabric and wool can be kept and used to make something lovely that they will really enjoy wearing. Recycling also plays a big part, too, as you can use fabric or buttons from old clothes; rummaging around for things to use can be an exciting part for your children. This was the part I really loved as a child.

Making jewellery is an excellent way for kids to express their individuality – they can jazz up a party dress with a cute sparkly brooch, or add a pretty corsage to a wedding outfit. But if they can bear to part with what they have made, many of the projects will serve well as Christmas and birthday gifts. So have fun making some eye-catching jewellery!

materials

Jewellery can be made from a huge variety of materials, but there are a few main items that are great to have at hand when starting out. Begin by collecting little items here and there to build up your jewellery and crafting kit.

beads

Beads come in a world of colours and shapes and are probably the most exciting part of making jewellery. It is always easy to get carried away when purchasing beads, especially at the beginning as there really is no end to what you can buy!

Chunky wooden beads are lovely for younger children's projects as they are big and bright and easy to use, with large holes for simple threading. Acrylic beads are also really versatile and come in a huge range of shapes and sizes. The faceted ones add a bit of sparkle and look fantastic.

As children get older, they can start to experiment with much smaller beads, such as seed beads, to make their jewellery more detailed.

ribbon

It is always good to have a selection of ribbon to hand when making jewellery. There is a huge selection to choose from. Simple satin ribbon is great as it comes in a wide variety of colours and widths, but also look around for patterned ribbons, such as spot or heart motifs, as these add some extra interest to your projects.

threads

You can thread beads onto a variety of materials – embroidery thread, nylon wire, elastic, leather or wax cord and ribbon are all good. A basic necklace can be made by simply knotting these onto a clasp and threading on beads. Equally, you can complete your item by simply tying the ends together.

buttons

Buttons come in a huge variety of shapes and sizes and add a sense of old-fashioned charm to jewellery work. Buy them individually, according to your taste, or in large assorted bags and see what you find. Big colourful buttons look great added to felt, while metal and enamelled buttons will give your projects a lovely vintage look.

fabric

Collect little pieces of fabric for your projects. Buy small amounts from a roll – even a quarter of a metre/yard will be ample for little projects – or cut up old clothes into small squares and keep them to use. Fabric with small prints works especially well for jewellery projects as the pattern is still distinguishable at a small scale.

felt

Felt is a fantastic material as it is so easy to work with, comes in every colour imaginable and is easily cut into shapes without the risk of fraying. It is perfect for children as they will love its texture and how quickly you can use it to make little items. A must-have for any budding crafter!

tools and findings

Although you do not need any specialist tools for the projects in this book, you will need a sturdy pair of scissors, capable of cutting through thin wire. If you will be going on to make lots of jewellery, you may want to buy a pair of wire cutters for cutting slightly thicker wire, which are available from all good craft suppliers. Large jump rings can be opened using your hands, but for smaller ones you may also need the help of a small pair of jewellery pliers, which are again available from craft suppliers and are relatively inexpensive. A variety of simple jewellery clasps can be bought from most large crafting suppliers, but many of the following projects are simply tied in a knot to finish.

techniques

There are some invaluable techniques that you will use time and time again in your jewellery making. Threading beads onto ribbon, sewing on a button, blanket stitch and plaiting are four techniques that are used in many of the projects throughout the book. Here are some helpful tips on how to achieve the best results.

threading beads onto ribbon

Sometimes it can be difficult to thread a wide ribbon through the hole of a bead, especially if it is a small bead. You can use a piece of thin elastic cord or jewellery wire to help you.

1 thread the elastic

Cut a short length of elastic cord about 10cm/4in long. If there is already a loop in the ribbon you need to thread, simply thread the elastic through the loop and fold in half so that you hold the ends of the elastic together. If it is a single piece of ribbon, create a loop in the ribbon and hold it in place with one hand while you loop the elastic cord through with the other.

2 pull through bead

Now use the elastic cord as a needle and simply thread the two ends through the bead. Keep pulling until the ribbon loop slips effortlessly through your bead. If the bead hole is too small for elastic cord, you can use thin jewellery wire in the same way, folding the wire in half to form a needle shape and using this to pull your ribbon through your bead.

sewing on a button

When crafting, you'll often find there is some point at which you have to sew on a button. Use this simple technique for stitching buttons firmly to your pretty jewellery projects.

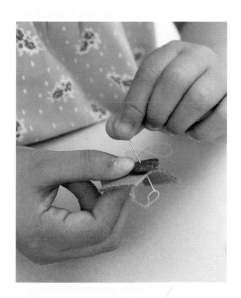

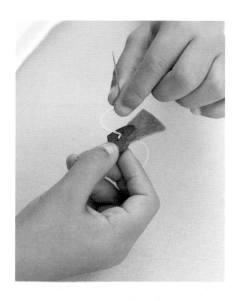

little tips

A good old-fashioned thimble can sometimes be useful, especially when sewing on lots of buttons. Ask an adult to help you with the initial positioning of your thimble and your button until you get the hang of it.

1 starting out

Thread your needle and sew a few small stitches through the fabric where the button needs to go, to hold the thread in place. Place the button on the fabric and pass the needle through the fabric and up through one of the button holes. Pull the thread all the way through and then pass the needle back down through the other button hole and through the fabric.

2 secure the button

Keep passing the needle through the two button holes, repeating five or six times until the button feels firm when tugged gently. Make sure the needle is at the back then sew a few small stitches in the fabric behind the button to secure. Cut off the excess thread with a pair of scissors.

blanket stitch

Blanket stitch is a great sewing technique that binds edges together neatly and securely. It is simple to do and works well for felt projects as the felt does not fray and gives you a nice finish.

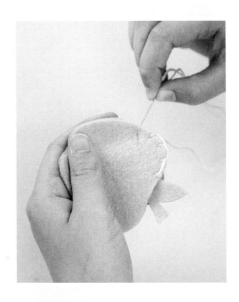

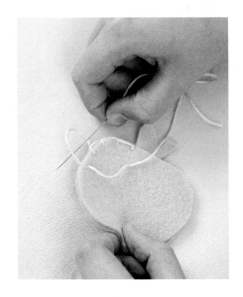

1 starting out

Thread your needle with embroidery thread (choose a colour that goes well with the felt as the stitches are very visible) and sew a couple of small stitches in the felt to start out. Now, take your needle and pass it through your piece of felt from front to back.

2 catch the loop

Don't pull the thread all the way through and you will be left with a loop. Take the needle over the top of the felt, passing it through the loop you have just made, and pull the needle gently to tighten the stitch. Place your needle a little further along the edge of the felt and repeat, pulling the needle back through the felt from front to back and catching the loop each time.

3 finishing

Continue in the same way all around your felt edge. When you have finished, make a double stitch to secure it and cut off the excess thread with a pair of scissors.

plaiting

Plaiting is a great technique to incorporate into your jewellery making. Embroidery thread works well for this, but you can also plait wool or satin ribbon and achieve lovely results.

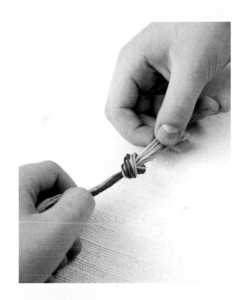

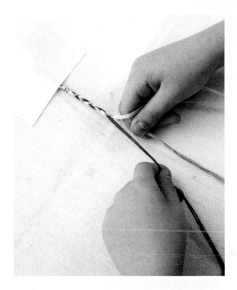

1 tie a knot

To plait, you will need three strands of thread of equal length. Tie a simple knot a few cm/in from the end to hold them together. You can plait single threads, or, if you want a thicker plait, plait several threads at once, but make sure that each section you are plaiting has an equal amount of threads or the plait may look uneven.

2 attach to a surface

To make the plaiting easier, use a piece of sticky tape above the knot to tape the threads to a work surface so that you get tension as you plait. Always make sure the tape will not ruin the surface you are working on. As an alternative you can place the threads under a heavy book.

3 plait the thread

The technique of plaiting is to pass each of the two outside threads over the centre one in turn to bind them all together. Begin with your right hand and pass the thread over the centre one – this will now become the centre thread. Take the left thread and pass it over the centre one. Repeat all the way down and tie the ends together in a knot at the bottom to secure.

Brilliant Beads

* pipe cleaner bracelets
* funky shoelace necklace
* glitter pasta necklace
* wooden shapes necklace
* leather alphabet bracelet
* rainbow button necklace
* stretchy button bracelet
* bracelet trio with ribbon
* beaded friendship bracelet
* wire heart pendant
* raffia and bead necklace
* wire bead bracelet
* lattice bracelet

pipe cleaner bracelets

Pipe cleaners are so versatile! By simply adding some big wooden beads they transform into bright chunky bracelets. Just make sure the bead holes are big enough to thread the pipe cleaner through.

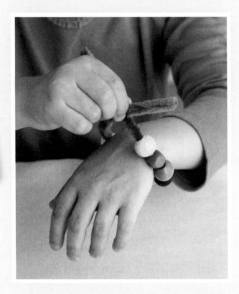

1 thread the beads

Choose your colour combination of pipe cleaner and beads. Thread the beads onto the pipe cleaner. It's nice to leave a bit of space between each bead so the brightly coloured pipe cleaner shows through.

2 measure the bracelet

Hold the pipe cleaner around your wrist to measure your size. Make sure you make it big enough to slip over your hand. Once you have the right length, twist the pipe cleaners together to secure the bracelet.

3 cut off the excess

Ask an adult to help you cut off the stray ends with a pair of scissors. Make sure that the scratchy ends are safely tucked inside the soft fluff of the pipe cleaner. Try making a few in various different colour combinations and wearing them all together.

you will need

pipe cleaners • assorted chunky wooden beads • scissors

funky shoelace necklace

Exciting patterned shoelaces, such as these spooky skulls, are great to turn into necklaces. The plastic coated ends make them easy for younger children to thread.

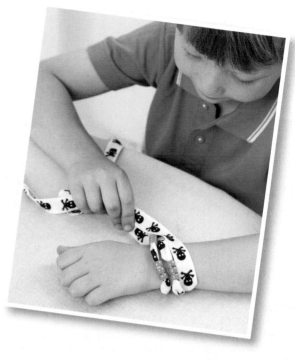

1 thread the beads

Lay your shoelace on a flat work surface and begin to thread on your beads. Experiment with the arrangement, grouping beads together and leaving a bit of space between the groups so the pattern of the shoelace shows through.

2 tie the shoelace

When you have threaded on all your beads, tie the ends of the shoelace together. You may need to ask an adult to help you with this.

3 try an alternative

If you want, you can make a bracelet from the shoelace by wrapping it around your wrist and then asking an adult to help tie a knot to secure it.

you will need

patterned or brightly coloured shoelace • about 20 plastic pony beads

glitter pasta necklace

This is a really fun project that younger children will love as it is so messy! Use larger size pasta as it is easier to thread and looks more impressive when it's coated in glitter.

1 cover pasta in glue

Pour the glue onto one of the plates and the glitter onto the other two, keeping the colours separate. Take a piece of pasta and roll it in the glue first, making sure you cover the whole surface of the pasta. This can be quite a messy job, so have some paper towels on standby!

2 coat in glitter

Take your glue-covered pasta and roll it in the glitter. Try to get a nice even coverage, without any gaps. Coat all of your pasta in this way, coating half in one colour glitter and half in the other. Leave them to dry.

3 thread the pasta

When the pasta is dry, take your length of ribbon and lay it on a flat work surface so the pasta doesn't fall off as you thread. Thread on the glittery pasta pieces, alternating between the two colours to get a stripy effect.

you will need

PVA/white glue • 3 plates (1 for glue and 2 for glitter) • glitter in 2 different colours • 12 pieces of large tubular pasta, such as penne or tortiglioni • paper towels • 80cm/32in satin ribbon

4 tie the ribbon

When you have finished threading,
ask an adult to help you tie the ends
of the ribbon together in a bow.

little tip

When PVA/white glue dries
it forms a hard plastic film
which can be easily peeled
off. However, it is always
best to use a disposable
paper plate or an old plate.
Try to avoid using plates
that you will eat off.

wooden shapes necklace

This simple necklace is great for practising threading. Try to thread the beads in an order so that they are symmetrical. Use interesting, attractive beads – animal shapes are perfect.

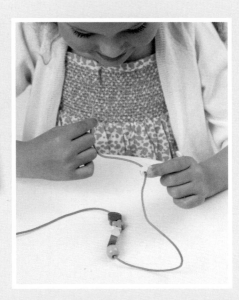

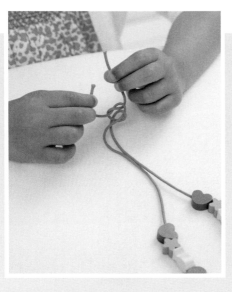

1 cut the cord

Measure and cut a length of cord for your necklace. Make sure that the necklace will be big enough to fit over your head when tied. It is a good idea to always cut at least 8cm/3in extra to allow for tying.

2 thread the beads

Lay the cord on a flat work surface so the beads do not fall off as you thread. Thread your beads onto the cord. Try to add the beads in an order that makes the necklace symmetrical.

3 tie the cord

When you have finished threading the beads, tie the ends of the cord together in several strong knots and trim off any excess with a pair of scissors. You may need to ask an adult to help you with this.

you will need

length of coloured cord (approximately 60cm/24in long) • scissors • assorted chunky wooden beads

rainbow button necklace

Thread lots of buttons on a cord to make a great necklace. You can group them together to give a great barrel effect which looks like rainbow stripes. Try adding in other plastic beads, too.

1 measure the elastic

Measure and cut a length of elastic for your necklace. Make sure that the necklace will be big enough to stretch over your head when tied. It is a good idea to always cut at least 8cm/3in extra to allow for tying.

2 add the buttons

Lay the elastic on a flat work surface so the buttons do not fall off as you thread. Start threading on the buttons, five at a time. Mix the colours together to get a lovely rainbow effect.

3 continue threading

Continue threading the necklace, mixing in the different sorts of beads with the groups of buttons as you go. When you have threaded half the length of the necklace, add a big bead, which will fall in the middle. From then on, thread the same order of beads but in reverse so that the necklace is symmetrical.

you will need

length of thin elastic cord (approximately 50cm/20in long) • scissors • assorted brightly coloured buttons • 8mm/$\frac{1}{3}$in plastic beads • assorted crystal acrylic and wooden beads

4 tie to finish

Tie the ends of the elastic together in several strong knots and trim off the excess with a pair of scissors. You may need to ask an adult to help you with this.

little tip

It's a good idea to use buttons with two holes rather than four as they are easier to thread onto the cord. To get the lovely barrel effect, use buttons that are all the same size.

stretchy button bracelet

These lovely colourful bracelets are so easy to make. Collect some pretty colour buttons and simply thread onto elastic. They look great when you make a few and wear them together.

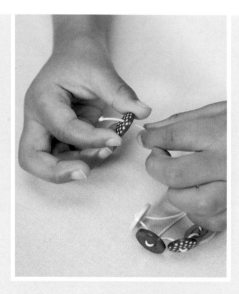

1 measure the elastic

Measure and cut a length of elastic for your bracelet. Make sure that the bracelet will be big enough to stretch over your hand when tied. It is a good idea to always cut at least 8cm/3in extra to allow for tying.

2 thread the buttons

Lay the elastic on a flat work surface so the buttons do not fall off as you thread. Start threading on the buttons. Make sure that you thread each button starting from the back so that they sit face up on the bracelet and you see any pattern they might have on them.

3 tie to finish

Tie the ends of the elastic together in several strong knots and trim off the excess with a pair of scissors. You may need to ask an adult to help you with this.

little tip

When making these bracelets, it's best to use buttons with two holes as they are much simpler to thread.

you will need

length of thin elastic cord (approximately 20cm/8in long) • scissors • assorted brightly coloured buttons

bracelet trio with ribbon

These bracelets can be made with a variety of beads. Choose colours you think look nice together and add ribbon in a complementary colour, finishing it with a pretty bow.

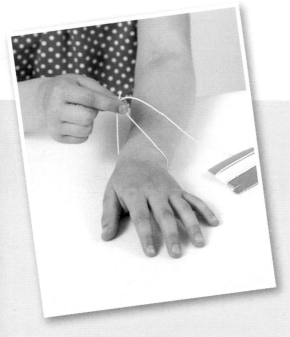

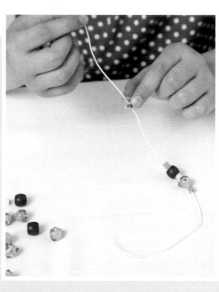

1 measure the elastic

Measure and cut a length of elastic for your bracelet. Make sure that the bracelet will be big enough to stretch over your hand when tied. It is a good idea to always cut at least 8cm/3in extra to allow for tying. Use this first length of elastic as a guide and cut two more of the same length.

2 thread the beads

Lay the elastic on a flat work surface so the beads do not fall off as you thread. Thread the beads onto the elastic. When you have finished threading, tie the two ends together in a tight knot and cut off the excess with a pair of scissors. Thread and finish the other two bracelets in the same way.

3 tie on the ribbon

When all three bracelets have been completed, group them together and thread your ribbon around them. Tie them together in a knot and finish with a bow.

you will need

length of thin elastic cord (approximately 70cm/28in long) • scissors • assorted glass or plastic beads • 15cm/6in satin ribbon

little tip

Try making one bracelet with all plain beads and two with mixed colours. This gives a nice contrast when all three bracelets are held together.

beaded friendship bracelet

Friendship bracelets have always been a firm jewellery favourite and make a lovely gift for all your friends and family. Try wearing a few bracelets together in a variety of colours.

1 cut the thread

Cut three pieces of each colour of embroidery thread 30cm/12in long. You should have nine pieces in total. Tie the pieces together leaving about 8cm/3in above the knot – this will be used to tie the bracelet onto the wrist.

2 plait in the beads

Attach the threads temporarily to a secure suface with sticky tape. Start to plait the bracelet, using the technique on page 13. As you plait, thread a bead onto one of the colour sections and continue plaiting. Continue to add the beads at regular intervals.

3 finishing

When you have only 8cm/3in of the thread left, stop plaiting and tie the nine threads together in a knot. Use the extra thread at either end of the plait to tie the bracelet around your friend's wrist and cut off the excess thread with a pair of scissors.

you will need

3 spools of embroidery thread in different colours • scissors • sticky tape • 3 pony beads • 2 plastic beads

wire heart pendant

All you need to make this necklace are some wire, beads and ribbon. By carefully manipulating the wire you can make it into a heart shape. Choose crystal colours to get that sparkly effect.

1 thread the beads

Lay the wire on a flat work surface so the beads do not fall off the wire as you thread. Thread the small beads onto the wire, leaving about 5cm/2in wire free at each end. When you have finished threading on your beads, bring the two ends together and twist the wires around each other a few times to secure. Cut off the excess wire.

2 form the heart

You should now have a beaded circle. To create the heart, push the join that you have just made into the middle of the circle to form the two arches at the top of the heart shape. Pinch the wire at the bottom of the heart together to form a point.

3 finishing

Take your satin ribbon and tie it onto the heart shape, between the two arches. The knot should fall in the middle of the ribbon so you have two equal lengths of ribbon on either side. Thread your large bead onto the ribbon using the technique on page 10. Tie the two lengths of ribbon together in a bow.

you will need

20cm/8in silver-plated wire (2mm/$\frac{1}{16}$in thick) • 26 small faceted beads plus 1 larger faceted bead in the same colour • scissors • 60cm/24in satin ribbon (3mm/$\frac{1}{8}$in wide)

raffia and bead necklace

Raffia is an easy material to use and gives a great rustic quality to jewellery. It comes in lots of different colours; you can go for the traditional sandy colour or try something different like this red.

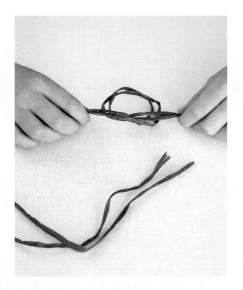

1 cut the raffia

Cut two equal lengths of raffia, each about 80cm/32in long. It's a good idea to cut a generous length of raffia as it gives you plenty to work with as the necklace will quickly become shorter as you thread and knot in your beads. You can always trim off the excess at the end. Knot together the two pieces of raffia about 8cm/3in from the end.

2 knot on the beads

Thread a bead through one length of the raffia and leave the other length to wrap around the outside of the bead. Knot the pieces of raffia together so the bead is held in place.

3 tie to finish

Continue threading on your beads to make up your necklace, knotting the rafia together after each bead. Stop when you have 8cm/3in of the raffia left. Tie the two ends together to complete your necklace.

you will need

1 reel of raffia • scissors • assorted chunky wooden beads

wire bead bracelet

This delicate bracelet is made by rolling thin wire around beads, creating an eye-catching effect. The technique is so simple and the result so beautiful, you will want to make a necklace, too.

1 attach the ring

Cut a piece of wire 25cm/10in long. Thread 2.5cm/1in of the wire through the toggle ring, then bend it and twist around the remaining wire to secure the ring in place.

2 start the wire ball

Cut another length of wire 1m/3ft long. Using circular motions, gently roll the wire in the palm of your hand to manipulate it into a ball shape.

3 add the bead

When the wire starts to look like a ball, drop a large bead into the middle and continue rolling until the wire is wrapped tightly around the bead. Wrap all of the seven large beads in this way.

little tip

This technique works best if you use brightly coloured beads, which will shine through the wire mesh. You can use softer coloured beads in between the wire beads – try using faceted ones to add some extra sparkle.

you will need

2 reels of thin wire (2mm/$\frac{1}{16}$in thick) • scissors • toggle clasp • 7 large beads • 8 smaller faceted beads

4 thread the beads

Lay the wire on a flat work surface so the beads do not fall off as you thread. Beginning with one of the smaller faceted beads, thread your beads onto the wire, alternating the large wire-wrapped beads with small ones to create a pretty effect.

5 attach the bar

When you have only 5cm/2in of wire remaining, stop threading beads and thread the toggle bar onto the end of the wire. Pull the wire taut, making sure the beads are all sitting snugly together with no gaps between them.

6 cut off the excess

Wrap the wire through the jump ring on the toggle bar a few times to secure it and then cut off the excess wire with a pair of scissors.

variation: wire bead necklace

To create a gorgeous necklace with your beads, simply replace the toggle clasp with two jump rings. Tie each end of a length of ribbon to each ring, adding a pretty bow detail to the necklace.

lattice bracelet

This is a fantastic weaving project using really simple materials. By experimenting with the order in which you thread the beads, you can create lots of different patterns and effects.

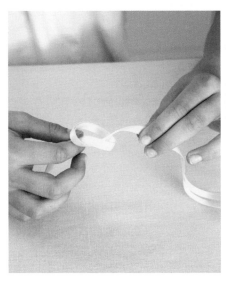

1 cut the ribbon

Cut two lengths of ribbon each 1m/ 3ft long. (This sounds like a lot for a bracelet, but as you thread the ribbon back and forth through the rows of beads, it will quickly be used up.)

2 tie the ribbon

Tie the ribbons together leaving about 8cm/3in above the knot – this will be used to tie the bracelet onto the wrist.

3 thread the beads

Take one length of the ribbon and thread on the first four pony beads. Use one bead of each colour, and push them all the way down the ribbon so they sit next to the knot.

you will need

1 reel of satin ribbon (5mm/¼in wide) • scissors • plastic pony beads in 4 different colours

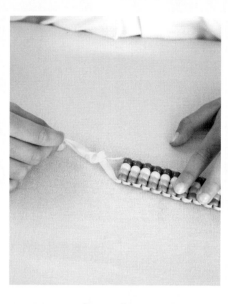

4 start to weave

Take the other length of ribbon and thread it back through the row of beads in the opposite direction. Tug the ribbons gently so that they are tight and the beads lie flat against the knot.

5 continue threading

Add the next four beads and repeat Step 4. Keep going until you have built up your bracelet. You can add the colours in the same order each time, or experiment with rotating the colours to make a zigzag pattern.

6 tie to finish

When you have threaded enough beads to make a bracelet long enough to fit your wrist, simply tie a strong knot in the ribbon. Cut off the excess ribbon, leaving 8cm/3in to tie the bracelet around your wrist with a bow.

variation: lattice belt

You can also use this technique to create a gorgeous belt, which looks great with jeans or slung around a tunic. You will need to start with two lengths of ribbon about 4m/13ft long, although this will depend on how many rows of beads you add.

Fabric Fashions

* hawaiian flower garland
* pirate pendant necklace
* pom pom necklace
* ribbon and bow necklace
* vintage apple and
  lace necklace
* fabric-wrapped bangles
* big flower brooch
* zigzag bracelets
* crafty felt flower pendant
* spiral bead necklace
* cupcake brooch
* fabric-wrapped bead necklace
* tassel bag charm

hawaiian flower garland

This bright, summery garland is made from drinking straws and fabric flowers, which are available in craft stores. This is a great project for younger children as the straws are easy to thread.

1 cut the straws

Cut the drinking straws into sections approximately 3cm/1¼in long. Begin with four or five straws and cut more if you find you need them.

2 start threading

Lay the elastic on a flat work surface so the decorations do not fall off as you thread. Start threading the necklace, beginning with a straw.

3 finishing

Continue to thread the decorations, in the following order: a straw, a pony bead, three flowers together, a pony bead, and then another straw. Repeat until the elastic is full, leaving approximately 8cm/3in elastic spare at either end. Tie the ends of the elastic together in a strong knot and trim off the excess with a pair of scissors. You may need to ask an adult to help you with this.

you will need

drinking straws in bright colours • scissors • 70cm/28in invisible elastic • pony beads • fabric flower petals

pirate pendant necklace

This pirate-inspired pendant was made by gluing felt to card. We added the skull and crossbones to cord to make a necklace, but you could also make it into a keyring by adding a keyring clasp.

1 cut the shape

Make a photocopy of the skull and crossbones template on page 114. Cut it out and place it on top of the black card. Draw around it with a pencil, using your other hand to hold the stencil in place. Carefully cut out the shape with scissors.

2 glue the felt

Add some glue to your cardboard shape and stick the sheet of black felt on top. When it has dried, cut the felt around the cardboard shape. Repeat on the other side of the card so that you have felt covering each side.

3 add the eyes

Cut two small circles from your grey felt to make the eyes and stick to the front of your skull and crossbones with a dab of glue. Make a hole at the top of the skull with a hole punch.

you will need

paper for template • scissors • 1 sheet of black card • pencil • PVA/white glue • 1 sheet of black felt • 1 sheet of grey felt • hole punch • 60cm/24in red cord

4 thread the cord

Tie the two ends of the cord together
so you have a loop. Thread 5cm/2in
of the loop through the hole from back
to front. Take the knot in your hand
and bring it over the top of the skull
and pass it through the loop at the
front of the card. Pull gently to tighten
the cord around the skull.

pom pom necklace

Pom poms look really striking when used for jewellery. They are soft and tactile and look really pretty. Simply use a piece of yarn for the actual necklace so there is no need for metal claps.

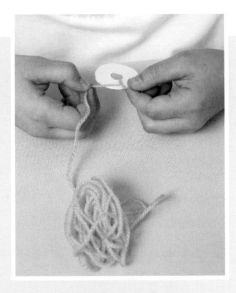

1 cut the wool

Cut a length of wool long enough to make a necklace. As you will not be using catches, make sure it will fit over your head comfortably. Cut another longer length of wool (about 1m/3ft) for the pom pom.

you will need

4 balls of wool in assorted colours • scissors • paper for template • pencil • 1 sheet of thick card • needle with a large eye

2 cut out template

Make a photocopy of the pom pom template on page 114. Cut it out and trace it onto the card twice with a pencil. Cut out the card ring – you may need to ask an adult to help you cut out the middle section. Put the two card rings together and begin to wrap the long length of wool around them.

3 wind the wool

Keep winding the wool around the cardboard ring, pulling it tightly as you go. Keep going until the whole template is covered with wool and the hole in the centre of the ring is completely full (you may have to use a needle towards the end to push the wool through the hole). If your wool runs out halfway through, simply add another length of wool and keep on wrapping.

4 cut around the edge

When you have finished winding the pom pom, use a needle to thread your necklace wool through the middle. Use scissors to cut around the edge of the card ring – the blade of the scissors should be able to slide between the two cardboard discs to snip the wool.

5 tie to secure

Take a short length of wool and wrap it between the two cardboard discs. Tie it tightly in a knot and then cut off the excess wool.

6 remove the card

Carefully peel away the templates, leaving the finished pom pom in place on the necklace. If you do this carefully you can re-use the template for your next pom pom.

variation: pom pom bag charm

When making up your pom poms, why not make up two or three extra? You can use them to make an exciting bag charm or keyring. Here we used the pom poms along with some beads knotted onto ribbon and attached them all to a keychain for a pretty accessory.

7 tie to finish

Tie the ends of wool together to finish.
The pom poms will move slightly on
the wool and you can position them
so that they are evenly spaced along
your necklace.

ribbon and bow necklace

This sweet necklace is made from little felt and button bows, sewn onto ribbon. Try using different shaped buttons, such as hearts and flowers. The bows and buttons could be glued on, if preferred.

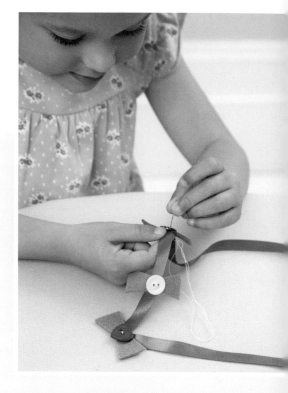

1 cut out the bows

Cut a rectangle of felt approximately 2.5cm/1in by 5cm/2in. Fold the rectangle in half and cut out a triangle from the middle – this will create a bow shape when flattened out. Make five bows in this way.

2 sew on the buttons

Using the needle and thread, sew a button in the middle of each bow, using the technique on page 11.

3 sew on the bows

Take your length of ribbon and fold it into a 'v' shape in the middle (this will help your necklace sit flat when you wear it). Sew a bow onto your ribbon at this point to mark the centre of the necklace. Continue sewing on the bows, adding two on either side.

you will need

2 sheets of coloured felt in different colours • scissors • needle • cotton thread • 5 assorted buttons • 60cm/24in satin ribbon (5mm/¼in wide)

4 tie to finish

Tie the two lengths of ribbon together in a bow to complete the necklace.

vintage apple and lace necklace

This gorgeous necklace was made using lengths of lace and ribbon and an apple motif made from felt. This is a great sewing project for practising skills such as blanket stitch and sewing on a button.

1 cut out the apples

Make a photocopy of the two apple templates on page 115. Carefully cut them out with scissors and place on top of the green felt. Draw around the templates with a pencil and then carefully cut out the apples.

2 sew on the buttons

Take the felt apple with the stalk and sew on four buttons with the cotton thread (using the technique on page 11) so that they look like apple seeds.

3 stitch the apple

Place the two apples together so that the seeds are on the outside. Using embroidery thread, sew the two apple shapes together using blanket stitch (using the technique on page 12).

you will need

paper for template • scissors • 1 sheet of green felt • pencil • scissors • 4 small buttons • needle • cotton thread • embroidery thread • 2 x 1m/3ft lengths of ribbon in different colours • 1m/3ft lace ribbon • pins

4 finishing

Lay your lengths of ribbon and lace on a flat work surface, making sure the ends all line up. Gather the ribbons together and pin on your apple, about one-third of the way down. Sew your apple onto the ribbons, making sure you catch the lace and both pieces of ribbon as you sew, so all the strands sit nicely together. Try to pass the needle through just the back of the apple, so the stitches aren't visible from the front. Tie the ends of the ribbon in a bow to complete your necklace.

fabric-wrapped bangles

Bring a plain bangle to life with some pretty fabric. Dainty floral cottons with a small pattern work really well. Try making a few using an assortment of designs and wear them together.

1 cut a fabric strip

Use your scissors to carefully cut a long strip of fabric, about 60cm/24in long and 2.5cm/1in wide.

2 attach to bangle

Take the end of your fabric strip and glue it to the inside of your bangle. Leave to dry for a few minutes.

3 wrap the fabric

Begin to wrap the fabric strip around the bangle, making sure it overlaps each time and that none of the plastic bangle is showing through. Continue wrapping until the entire bangle is covered with fabric.

you will need

scissors • length of patterned fabric (at least 60cm/24in long) • plastic bangle • glue stick

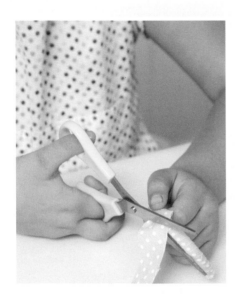

little tip

A slightly frayed edge to the fabric can give your bangles a vintage feel, so you can skip the trimming stage if you wish. Alternatively, you could use pinking shears to cut the length of fabric. This will prevent fraying and also give an interesting crinkly effect.

4 cut off the excess

When you have finished wrapping the bangle, cut off the excess fabric, leaving about 2.5cm/1in spare to apply the glue to.

5 glue down the end

Apply plenty of glue to the end of the fabric strip and stick it to the inside of the bangle so it is invisible when you are wearing it. Trim off any stray bits of cotton that may have frayed during the wrapping process. Wear the bangle on its own or make a few and tie them together with a pretty ribbon.

variation: fabric-wrapped hairband

You can use the same technique to make a gorgeous hairband. Here we used the same pretty polka dot fabric and added a vibrant pink organza ribbon bow. Use a reasonably wide hairband so that you can really see the fabric.

big flower brooch

Mix pretty patterned fabric and plain felt to make this stunning flower brooch. It looks great pinned to a party dress or make it in wintery colours and pin it to your coat.

1 cut out flowers

Make a photocopy of the five flower templates on pages 116–117 and carefully cut them out with scissors. Place the smallest flower template onto a sheet of felt and draw around it with a pencil, then cut out the shape. Lay the template for the second-smallest flower on a piece of fabric, draw around it in pencil and cut it out. Continue drawing and cutting the flowers in size order, alternating between the felt and fabric, until you have all five.

2 build the flower

Arrange the flower shapes on top of each other in size order to make a layered effect, then pin them together.

3 sew on the button

Place the button in the middle of the flower and use your needle and thread to sew it in place using the technique on page 11. Make sure you sew through all five layers of the flower so it is stitched together. Remove the pins.

you will need

paper for templates • scissors • 2 sheets of felt in different colours • pencil • 2 squares of patterned cotton fabric • pins • 1 large button • needle • cotton thread • brooch back • PVA/white glue

4 glue on the pin

To complete the brooch, stick the brooch pin to the back of the flower with a dab of glue. Leave it to dry completely before wearing.

zigzag bracelets

By plaiting old-fashioned rickrack trim together, you can make these exciting bracelets. This simple project is a great way to start experimenting with using jewellery findings.

1 cut the trim

Cut three pieces of rickrack 20cm/8in long, one in each of the different colours. Wrap a piece of sticky tape around the ends to hold the three pieces of rickrack together.

2 plait the rickrack

Attach the ends to a secure suface and start to plait the rickrack, using the technique on page 13. Use the zigzag shape as a guide for your plaiting, the trims should slot comfortably into each other. When you get to the end of the rickrack, wrap more sticky tape around the ends to hold them together.

3 glue on end caps

Place one taped end into a bracelet end cap. If the sticky tape shows beyond the end cap, trim a little bit off the end so that the strip of tape is narrow enough to be hidden inside the cap. Repeat with the other end so you have a neat finish. Squeeze glue into the end cap and insert one end of the plait into the cap. Allow the glue to dry a little and go sticky before gluing the other end of the bracelet into the other end cap in the same way. Leave the glue to dry for at least two hours until it is completely set.

you will need

rickrack trim in 3 different colours • scissors • sticky tape • 2 bracelet end caps • strong/tacky glue • jump ring • bracelet catch

4 attach the catch

Use the jump ring to attach the
bracelet catch to one of the end
caps. You can ask an adult to help
you do this with a pair of pliers, but
you may find the jump ring is soft
enough to open and close by hand.

crafty felt flower pendant

Flowers always look pretty as items of jewellery. This flower can be made in any colour you wish: felt comes in a huge array of beautiful colours from dazzling yellows to jewel-like emerald.

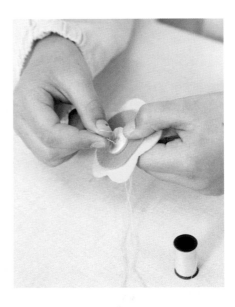

1 cut out flower

Make a photocopy of the templates on page 118 and carefully cut them out with scissors. Place each template onto a piece of felt (in the colour of your choice) and draw around it with a pencil. Carefully cut out the shapes. Cut out an extra small rectangle of felt the same colour as the leaf, and set aside.

2 build the flower

Arrange the felt shapes so that the leaf is at the bottom, then the large flower shape, and then the circle on top, and pin them together.

3 sew together

Place the button in the middle of the flower and use your needle and thread to sew it in place using the technique on page 11. Make sure you sew through all three layers of the flower so it is stitched firmly together. Remove the pins.

you will need

paper for templates • scissors • 3 sheets of coloured felt in different colours • pencil • pins • 1 pretty button • needle • cotton thread • 60cm/24in satin ribbon (3mm/⅛in wide) • PVA/white glue • 2 small wooden beads

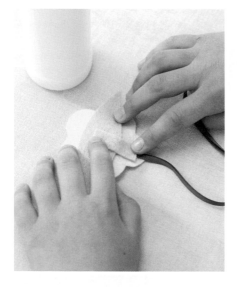

4 glue on the ribbon

Turn the flower over. Fold the length of ribbon in half and place the fold on the back of the flower. Take the extra rectangle of felt you cut and cover it with glue. Stick the felt onto the back of the flower, covering the ribbon, and leave to dry.

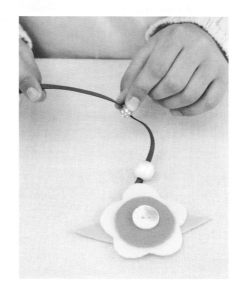

5 thread on the beads

Thread your beads onto the ribbon using the bead threading technique on page 10.

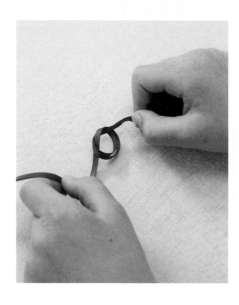

6 tie to finish

Simply tie the two ends of the ribbon together to complete the necklace.

variation: crafty felt flower headband

You can add your flower to lots of different items. Try stitching it onto a plain fabric hairband and wearing it in your hair (see page 46), or using the band to decorate a hat.

spiral bead necklace

Rolling felt together makes these wonderful beads. They can be used to make a variety of jewellery projects. Here we used them to make a necklace and added some chunky wooden beads too.

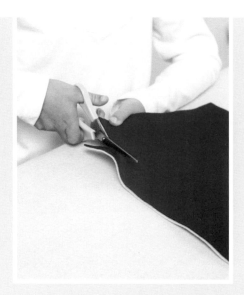

1 glue the felt

Take your six sheets of coloured felt and pair them up, deciding which colours should go together – you should have three pairs. Take the first pair and apply glue all over the surface of one of the felt sheets. Place the other sheet on top and smooth down firmly with your hands to make sure there are no creases or bubbles. Stick the other pairs together in the same way and leave them all to dry.

2 cut the strips

When the felt is dry, cut all the sheets lengthways into long strips about 1cm/½in wide.

3 sew the ends

Take each felt strip and roll it tightly to make a coil. Take a needle and cotton thread and secure the spiral felt bead by sewing down the end of the felt strip with a few small stitches.

you will need

6 sheets of felt in different colours • glue stick • scissors • strong needle • cotton thread • 70cm/28in embroidery thread • assorted chunky wooden beads

4 thread on the beads

Thread the beads onto the embroidery thread using a needle. Alternate between felt and wooden beads. Leave 8cm/3in thread free at each end for tying.

5 tie to finish

Simply tie the two ends of the thread together to complete the necklace.

cupcake brooch

A great 3D project to make, this eye-catching brooch includes sewing and beading. It looks cute on both denim jackets and hand-knitted woolly cardigans.

1 cut out the cake

Make a photocopy of the templates on page 119 and carefully cut them out with scissors. Place the templates onto the felt and stripy fabric and draw around with a pencil before carefully cutting out. You will need the frosting and one whole cupcake in felt and one whole cupcake in the stripy fabric.

2 glue on the icing

Using a few dabs of fabric glue, stick the frosting onto the stripy cupcake. Leave to dry for a few minutes.

3 sew on sprinkles

Take your needle and some cotton thread and sew your crystal beads onto the frosting in a scattered way, so they look like cake sprinkles.

you will need

paper for templates • scissors • 2 sheets of felt in different colours • 1 square of stripy fabric • pencil • fabric glue • needle • cotton thread • crystal seed beads • embroidery thread • wadding • 1 red button • strong/tacky glue • brooch pin

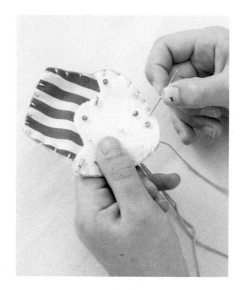

4 stitch around cake

Sew the front and back pieces of the cupcake together with embroidery thread, using the blanket stitch technique on page 12. Leave a gap of about 6cm/2½in.

5 add the wadding

Stuff the wadding through the gap to plump out the cupcake then finish sewing it up. Sew your button at the top of the cake, using the technique on page 11, so it looks like a cherry.

6 attach the pin

Use a dab of strong/tacky glue to attach your brooch pin. Leave to dry completely before wearing.

variation: heart brooches

We made these pretty heart-shaped brooches using the same technique. Tie a bow with some ribbon and place it under the button. You can wear them on your winter coat or add them to your party outfit.

fabric-wrapped bead necklace

Transform simple beads by covering them in pretty fabric. This is a fantastic project for using up material from old clothes or off-cuts found at your local haberdashery shop. Make each bead in a different patterned fabric to create a vintage feel.

1 tie on the toggle

Tie one end of the cord to either the ring or bar of the toggle clasp. Secure with a double knot and cut off the excess cord.

2 cut fabric strips

With your scissors, cut small strips of fabric long enough to cover one of the large beads from top to bottom.

3 glue on the material

Take a strip of material and cover it with glue. Starting at the top, wrap the glued strip around a large bead and smooth over to remove any creases. Continue to add strips until the whole bead is covered, taking care not to glue fabric over the bead hole. Cover all of the large beads in this way and leave them to dry completely.

you will need

50cm/20in coloured cotton cord • toggle clasp • scissors • scraps of fabric in different patterns and colours • glue stick • 7 large wooden beads • assorted small round and barrel-shaped wooden beads

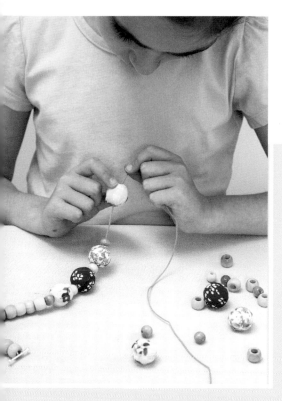

4 thread the beads

Start threading beads onto your cord, beginning with several small wooden beads. Begin to thread on the fabric-wrapped beads, alternating with the smaller beads. Once all the fabric-wrapped beads are threaded, finish by threading another section of the smaller beads. Tie the second piece of the toggle fastening to the cord to complete the clasp, and cut off the excess cord.

tassel bag charm

This is a fun accessory that you can make using scraps of fabric. Try mixing bold patterns and plain fabric together and add some colourful beads to really make it stand out.

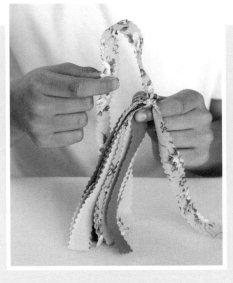

1 cut strips of fabric

Use the pinking shears to cut three strips of fabric from each piece. Each strip should be approximately 25cm/10in long and 2cm/¾in wide. Cut one extra strip of fabric about 40cm/16in long.

2 tie strips together

Lie the fabric strips on top of each other flat on the table. Find the middle and use the longer strip to tie all the strips together.

3 make the loop

Fold the strips in half so the ends all sit together. Take one half of the longer strip and make it into a long loop (making sure it is long enough to accommodate two beads). Hold in place and wrap the other half of the strip around to hold it in place.

you will need

pinking shears • 4 pieces of assorted cotton fabric • 2 big wooden beads • metal jump ring • bag charm attachment

4 secure bead loop

Tie the two ends of the longer strip together to secure the loop. Cut off the excess fabric.

5 thread on beads

Thread the beads onto the loop of fabric, using the technique on page 10.

6 attach bag clip

Take the jump ring and thread it through the loop at the top of the beads. Loop the bag charm attachment onto the jump ring and close the ring as tightly as possible.

variation: tassel necklace

To create a pretty necklace from the tassle, thread a cord or ribbon through the top of the loop in place of the jump ring. String some extra beads and attach jewellery fastenings to the ends of the cord.

Modelling Magic

* twinkling star brooch
* bright-as-a-button hair slide
* fuzzy dinosaur badge
* crystal butterfly necklace
* flower corsage brooch
* jigsaw keyring
* colourful clay pendant
* camouflage button belt
* candy bracelet

twinkling star brooch

Air-drying clay is so easy and fun to use. This colourful star brooch was shaped using a cookie cutter. Once dry, we painted it and added some star-like sparkle.

1 roll the clay

Cover a work surface with parchment paper. This will protect the surface as well as prevent the clay from sticking. Take a lump of clay from your block and roll it flat with your rolling pin. It needs to be about 5mm/¼in thick.

2 cut out the shape

Using your cookie cutter, cut out the star shape. Leave the shape to dry. This can take up to 24 hours, but placing the star somewhere warm will speed up the drying time.

3 paint the star

Make sure the star is completely dry then paint on a generous layer of poster paint. You may need to let the star dry and then apply a second coat of paint for complete coverage.

you will need

parchment paper • white air-drying clay • rolling pin • star cookie cutter • poster paint in 2 colours • paintbrush • PVA/white glue • flower diamanté • brooch pin

4 paint on spots

When the paint has dried, use the second colour of paint to add dots all over the star. Leave the star to dry.

5 add the diamanté

Dab a small blob of glue in the middle of the star to stick the diamanté motif in place. Leave to dry.

6 finishing

Glue your brooch pin to the back of the star and leave to dry before wearing proudly!

variation: animal brooches

There are lots of different cookie cutter shapes to choose from so you can really have fun making all sorts of brooches. Here we chose some animal shapes, painted them in bright colours and added a little diamanté for decoration. Roll the clay so that the brooches are a good thickness. This way they are less likely to snap and will last longer.

bright-as-a-button hair slide

Jazz up a plain hair slide by adding felt and bright buttons. See what buttons you have around the house, take them from old clothes or even hunt for them in your local charity shop.

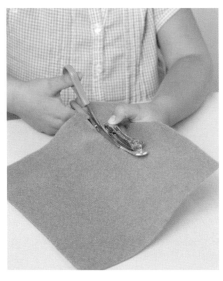

1 apply the glue

Hold the underside of the hair slide in one hand and use the other hand to apply glue to the flat surface of the slide with the glue stick. You will need quite a thick layer.

2 stick on the felt

Press the felt onto the glued surface of the hair slide and leave to dry. When dry, use scissors to cut around the hair slide shape.

3 add the buttons

Decide which order you would like your buttons in, laying them out on a flat work surface. Starting from one end, apply a dab of glue to the felt surface and stick on the first button. Continue to apply glue and buttons along the length of the hair slide. Leave to dry completely before wearing.

you will need

plain hair slides • glue stick • 1 sheet coloured felt • scissors • assorted plastic buttons • PVA/white glue

fuzzy dinosaur badge

Use sturdy card and patterned gift wrap to make this cute dinosaur badge. A googly eye and spots of fuzzy felt add the perfect finishing touches!

1 glue on gift wrap

Use your glue stick to coat the card in glue. Place your gift wrap on the glued surface, patterned side up, and smooth it down with your hands to make sure there aren't any bubbles. Leave to dry for a few minutes.

2 draw dinosaur

Make a photocopy of the dinosaur template on page 120. Cut it out and place it on top of the card. Draw around it with a pencil, using your other hand to hold the stencil in place.

3 cut out dinosaur

Carefully cut out the dinosaur shape with your scissors.

you will need

glue stick • 1 sheet of card • patterned gift wrap • paper for template • scissors • pencil • small scraps of felt in 2 different colours • PVA/white glue • 1 googly eye • brooch pin

5 glue on the eye

Put a dab of glue on the head of the dinosaur and stick on the googly eye.

4 add the spots

Take your scraps of felt and cut out small circles, about 5mm/¼in in diameter. You will need four or five of each colour. Use small dabs of glue to stick the spots on the dinosaur.

6 stick on the pin

Glue the brooch pin onto the back of the dinosaur with a dab of glue. Leave to dry completely before wearing.

variation: patterned animal badges

You can create all kinds of animals using the same technique. Here we made a giraffe and a crocodile to add to the animal collection. You can find templates for these on pages 120–121.

crystal butterfly necklace

This pretty sparkly necklace is simple to make and is a great piece to wear for a special occasion. Choose your favourite colour card to make the butterfly and go wild with the sparkles!

1 draw the butterfly

Make a photocopy of the butterfly template on page 122. Cut it out and place it on top of the card. Draw around it with a pencil, using the other hand to hold the stencil in place.

2 cut out butterfly

Cut out the butterfly shape with your scissors. Use the hole punch to make a hole at the top of the butterfly, between the two antennae.

3 add the crystals

Use small dabs of glue to stick on some pretty sparkly shapes. You could add the crystals randomly or decorate with a pattern in mind. Leave the glue to dry completely.

you will need

paper for template • scissors • coloured card • pencil • hole punch • PVA/white glue • 5–10 crystal sparkles • 60cm/24in coloured cord

4 thread the cord

Tie the two ends of the cord together so you have a loop. Thread 5cm/2in of the loop through the hole from front to back. Take the knot in your hand and bring it over the top of the butterfly and pass it through the loop on the other side of the card. Pull gently to tighten the cord around the butterfly.

flower corsage brooch

Tissue paper is a great material to work with and these big fun flowers really make an impact. Pick the brightest, dazzling colour tissue paper and add a motif in the middle to finish them off.

1 cut the tissue paper

Take your sheet of tissue paper and cut it in half lengthways. Lay the two halves on top of each other and fold them in half lengthways then cut down the crease so that you have four separate sections.

2 fold the paper

Place the sheets of paper on a flat work surface with the shortest edge closest you. Fold your paper concertina-style in folds that are 2cm/¾in wide. Press each fold flat.

3 cut the petal shape

Using your scissors, round off the corners by cutting a gentle curve across the tissue paper. Repeat at the other end of the tissue paper to form the petal shapes.

you will need

1 sheet of tissue paper • scissors • pipe cleaner • strong/tacky glue • brooch pin • small paper craft flower

4 tie paper in middle

Hold your tissue paper and wrap a pipe cleaner around the middle. Try to pull as tightly as possible so the paper is squeezed up in the middle. Twist the pipe cleaner together to secure.

5 pull out petals

Make the flower shape by slowly pulling the sections of tissue paper out. Do this gently to avoid ripping the paper. When you have fluffed out all the petals to make your flower, cut off the excess pipe cleaner.

6 finishing

Use strong/tacky glue to stick the brooch pin to the back of your flower and leave to dry. Turn the flower over and glue your paper flower motif in the middle of the flower to finish it off.

variation: flower corsage bracelet

Why not make your flower brooch into a bracelet? Pin your flower onto a length of satin ribbon and tie it around your wrist. These flowers look lovely for special occasions. Use gentle colours like white, pink or powder blue for bridesmaids or bright and lively colours to complement your party outfit.

jigsaw keyring

Ever wondered what to do with those odd jigsaw pieces? Find a piece with an interesting image and use it as it is, or cover it with some decorative gift wrap to create this quirky keyring.

1 draw around jigsaw

Place your jigsaw piece on top of the gift wrap and trace around it using your pencil. Make sure you draw on the patterned side of the decorative paper so that it fits the shape of the jigsaw piece.

2 cut the paper

Cut out the jigsaw shape from the paper. Cut the shape as carefully as you can so that it fits well over your jigsaw piece.

3 glue paper down

Coat the jigsaw piece in glue and then place the decorative paper on top, being careful to line it up with the jigsaw piece so you have a clean edge. Smooth it down with your hands, making sure there are no bubbles or creases in the paper, then leave the piece to dry completely.

you will need

large jigsaw piece • decorative paper or gift wrap • pencil • scissors • glue stick • strong hole punch • large jump ring • keychain

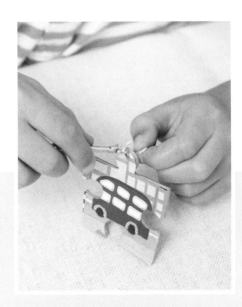

4 attach the keychain

Ask an adult to help you punch a hole in the jigsaw piece and thread through the jump ring. Large jump rings can be opened and closed with your hands or using a small pair of pliers. Thread on the keychain and close the jump ring to secure.

little tip

A strong hole punch can be found in all good craft shops and haberdashers. The punch used in this project can be used to make holes in belts and is also tough enough to go through a thick cardboard jigsaw piece. Ask an adult to help you punch the hole.

colourful clay pendant

By rolling or twisting different coloured modelling clay together, you can make these fun chunky pendants and beads.

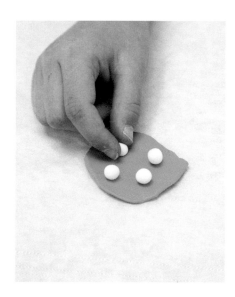

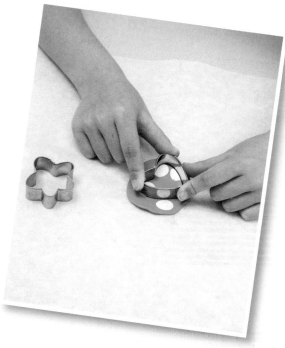

1 roll the clay

Cover a work surface with parchment paper. This will protect the surface as well as prevent the clay from sticking. Take a piece of clay and roll it flat with your rolling pin. It needs to be about 3mm/⅛in thick.

2 make the pattern

Roll small balls of clay in a contrasting colour. They should be a little smaller than a pea. Place them on top of the flat piece of clay and then roll over the surface with your rolling pin so the clays merge to create spots.

3 cut the pendant

Place your cookie cutter on the clay and push it down firmly to cut out the heart shape. Make a hole at the top of the heart with the wooden skewer and place it on the lined baking sheet.

you will need

parchment paper • modelling clay (such as Fimo) in at least 2 different colours • rolling pin • heart shaped cookie cutter • wooden skewer • baking sheet lined with parchment paper • 50cm/20in satin ribbon (3mm/⅛in wide)

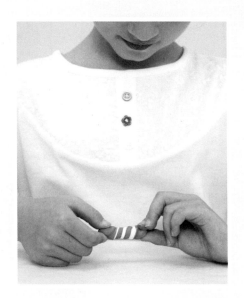

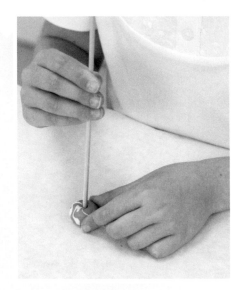

4 create the stripy bead

To make the stripy bead, take two small pieces of clay in different colours (you can repeat the colours you used for the pendant or use completely different colours) and roll them each into a small log. Press the logs together and, holding at either end, twist the logs together to create a spiral effect.

5 bake the clay

Take a lump of the stripy clay and, using circular motions, roll it in the palms of your hands to form a ball. Punch a hole through the middle of the ball with the wooden skewer and place on the baking sheet with the heart. Ask an adult to help you bake the clay shapes, following the manufacturer's instructions.

6 thread the ribbon

When the baked pendant and bead have cooled, take your length of satin ribbon and thread it through the heart shape and then add on your stripy bead. Tie the ends of the ribbon together to complete the necklace.

variation: clay bead necklace

You can make up lots of clay beads and turn them into a necklace. We mixed white with other bright colours to give that swirly effect, but you can mix other colours together, too, like red and orange and pink and blue. Experiment and see what you come up with.

camouflage button belt

This is a great way to liven up a simple belt. Make sure you buy a belt with plenty of space to sew on the clay buttons. Make them big and chunky so that they really stand out.

1 mix the colour

Lay a sheet of parchment paper on your work surface to protect it. Take two pieces of clay, one in each colour, and roll and twist them together to make the camouflage effect.

2 make the buttons

Roll out the clay with a rolling pin until it is about 3mm/⅛in thick. Take your cookie cutters and cut out an oval and a star shape. Place the star shape on top of the oval.

3 add button holes

Make two holes in the button using the wooden skewer. Make sure the holes go all the way through the button so the needle and thread can pass through. Repeat Steps 2 and 3 until you have enough buttons to run the length of the belt. Place the buttons on the lined baking sheet and ask an adult to help you bake the clay shapes, following the manufacturer's instructions.

you will need

parchment paper • modelling clay (such as Fimo) in khaki green and brown • rolling pin • oval- and star-shaped cookie cutters • wooden skewer • baking sheet lined with parchment paper • needle • embroidery thread • scissors • belt

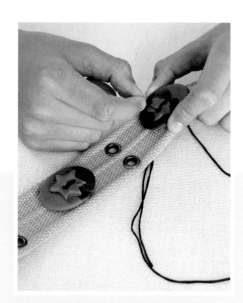

4 stitch on buttons

When the baked buttons have cooled, use a needle and thread to sew the buttons onto your belt, using the technique on page 11. Add as many as you like, remembering to leave enough room for the belt to loop through and buckle comfortably.

little tip

Only use items kept for modelling when working with clay. Never use items from the kitchen that are used for food. Always protect your work surface with a sheet of parchment paper as the colour from the clay can transfer onto surfaces and stain them.

candy bracelet

Make these cute bracelets from modelling clay – it's so easy to use. Here we have made some well-known liquorice candies and simply threaded them together with brilliant results!

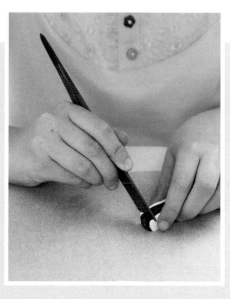

1 slice the clay

Lay a sheet of parchment paper on your work surface to protect it. Take a new block of clay (it's better to work straight from the block so that you always get a nice clean edge) and your modelling tool and carefully cut a slice of clay about 3mm/⅛in thick. Cut several slices from each coloured block of clay.

2 sandwich together

Sandwich the slices together and press down gently so that the slices stick to each other in small stacks.

3 trim off the ends

Take each stack of clay slices and trim off each end so that the candy becomes a square shape and the edges are lined up neatly.

you will need

parchment paper • modelling clay (such as Fimo) in black, purple, turquoise yellow and white • clay modelling tools • baking sheet lined with parchment paper • thin elastic cord (approximately 25cm/10in long) • scissors

4 vary the candies

To make the round candy, roll a log of coloured clay, about 2.5cm/1in thick. Use your modelling tool to cut off the end of the log so you have a nice flat surface to begin, and then cut the log into slices, about 1cm/½in thick. Place a slice between your thumb and forefinger and gently squeeze, so that each side of the slice is lightly indented. Place a small ball of black clay in one of these indents, and press lightly until it sticks and the black ball is flattened out to fill the indent. Turn over and repeat on the other side to create the effect that the black clay has passed through the middle of the coloured clay cylinder.

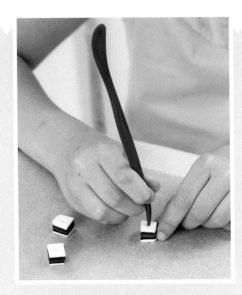

5 make the hole

Make a hole through the centre of the candy beads using the modelling tools. Make sure the holes go all the way through the beads so the elastic cord can pass through. Place the beads on the lined baking sheet and ask an adult to help you bake the clay shapes, following the manufacturer's instructions.

6 thread the beads

Measure and cut a length of elastic cord for your bracelet. Make sure that the bracelet will be big enough to stretch over your hand when tied. It is a good idea to always cut at least 8cm/3in extra to allow for tying. When the baked beads have cooled, thread them onto your elastic cord.

variation: candy hair clips

If you have a few candy beads left over, you could use them to make these pretty hair clips. Simply stick the beads onto plain or patterned hair clips using strong/tacky glue.

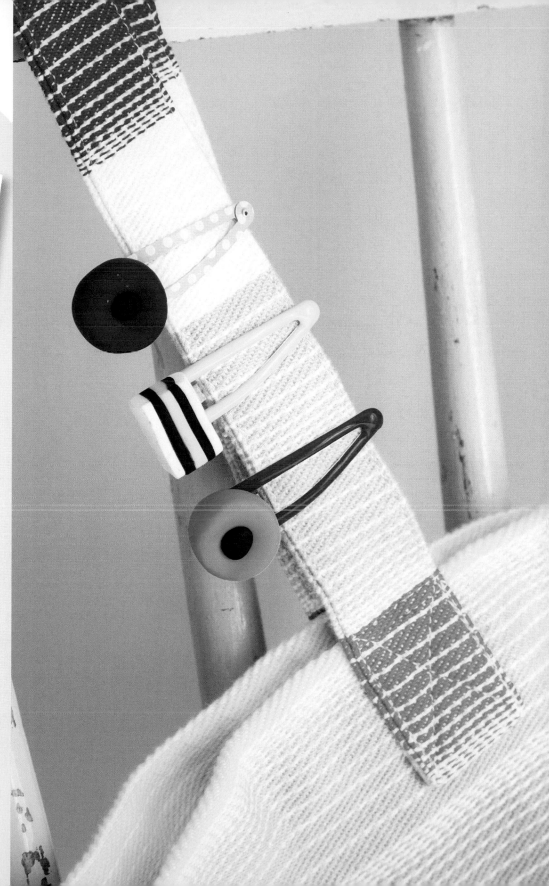

7 tie to finish

When you have finished threading
the beads, tie the ends of the elastic
cord together with several strong
knots and trim off the excess using
a pair of scissors.

templates

Use these templates to help with the projects pictured. They are all drawn at the correct size, so simply photocopy and cut out.

pom pom necklace
p52

pirate pendant necklace
p50

vintage apple and
lace necklace

p58

big flower brooch

p64

crafty felt flower pendant

p68

heart brooch

p76

cupcake brooch

p74

fuzzy dinosaur badge

p92

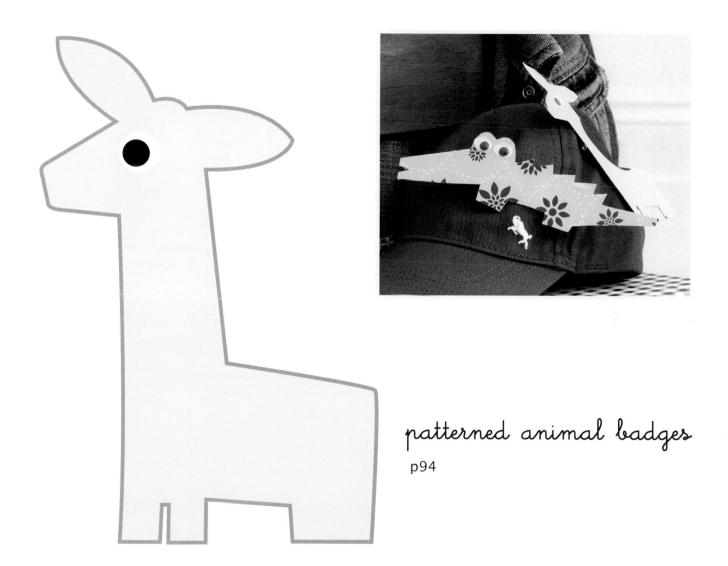

patterned animal badges

p94

crystal butterfly necklace

p96

resources

uk sources

BAKER ROSS

www.bakerross.co.uk

Large online retailer of kid's crafting materials. Great for big bags of assorted beads and packs of coloured felt. They also stock air-drying and modelling clay.

BIJOUX BEADS

www.bijouxbeads.co.uk

Online retailer with an extensive selection of more unusual beads and numerous options of ribbon, wire and cord to thread them onto.

THE BUTTON COMPANY

www.thebuttoncompany.co.uk

Online retailer that stocks a large range of buttons. Wood, plastic and shell buttons in various shapes and sizes, available to buy individually or in value bags.

THE BUTTON QUEEN

76 Marylebone Lane

London W1U 2PR

0207 935 1505

www.thebuttonqueen.co.uk

Stock a huge array of buttons from pearl and wood to colourful plastic.

CLAIRE'S ACCESSORIES

Visit www.claires.com *for your nearest store.*
For fabric headbands, plastic headbands and bangles, and hair clips.

THE COTTON PATCH

www.cottonpatch.co.uk

Online retailer selling a huge selection of fabrics that are great for crafting projects. You can buy them by the metre or in smaller squares.

COVENT GARDEN BEAD SHOP

21a Tower Street

London WC2H 9NS

020 7240 0931

www.beadworks.co.uk

Sell glass beads in an array of beautiful colours as well as wooden, plastic and metal beads. You can browse through their store in London or buy online.

CREATIONS ART AND CRAFT MATERIALS

01326 555777

www.creativebeadcraft.co.uk

Online craft store with a large stock of buttons, decorative fabric motifs, cord, ribbon and elastic.

CREATIVE BEADCRAFT

1 Marshall Street

London W1F 9BA

020 7734 1982

www.creativebeadcraft.co.uk

Stock a great selection of beads, ranging from glass to acrylic as well as jewellery cord and wire and all jewellery findings like clasps and jump rings. They also stock a range of jewellery tools.

EARLY LEARNING CENTRE

Visit www.elc.co.uk *for your nearest store.*
Stock a wide range of arts and crafts materials for younger children, including paints, glue, glitter, air-drying clay, felt, tissue paper and googly eyes.

HOBBYCRAFT

Visit www.hobbycraft.co.uk *for your nearest store.*
Crafts retailer stocking a large selection of beads plus felt, wool, decorative papers and modelling clay. You can also find adhesive diamanté stones and craft flowers.

HOMECRAFTS DIRECT

0116 269 7733

www.homecrafts.co.uk

Online retailer stocking a huge selection of craft materials, from beads and cords and jewellery findings, to modelling clay and fabrics.

JOHN LEWIS

Visit www.johnlewis.com
for your nearest store.
*Stocks a large selection of
haberdashery materials
including beads, needles,
rickrack trim, wool, fabrics and
satin ribbon. They also sell
cookie cutters.*

KIDZCRAFT

www.kidzcraft.co.uk
*Large online retailer of a huge
variety of craft materials.
Especially good for big bags of
brightly-coloured beads.*

PAPERCHASE

Visit www.paperchase.co.uk
for your nearest store.
*Stockists of a wide range of
tissue paper and gift wrap.*

TOYDAY TOYSHOP

www.toyday.co.uk
*Old fashioned wooden alphabet
beads and traditional toys.*

THE TRIUMPH PRESS

91 High Street
Edgware HA8 7DB
0208 951 3883
www.artclub.co.uk
*Large art materials supplier
where you can find beads,
felt, raffia and paint.*

WHSMITHS

Visit www.whsmiths.co.uk for
your nearest store.
*Stock a large selection of
crafting materials, including
good-quality glitter, glue and
packs of coloured cardboard.*

VV ROULEAUX

102 Marylebone Lane
London W1U 2QD
020 7224 5179
www.vvrouleaux.com
*An Aladdin's cave full of trims,
ribbons and feathers.*

us sources

A.C. MOORE
Visit www.acmoore.com for your nearest store.
Craft superstores carrying beads and jewellery kits, ribbons, sewing supplies, boutique buttons and modelling clay.

BRITEX FABRICS
146 Geary Street
San Francisco, CA 94108
415-392-2910
www.britexfabrics.com
Stock a wide range of novelty buttons, ribbons and fabric as well as general haberdashery supplies.

THE BUTTON EMPORIUM & RIBBONRY
1016 SW Taylor Street
Portland, OR 97205
503-228-6372
www.buttonemporium.com
Vintage and assorted decorative buttons and a huge range of ribbon.

CRATE FOR LESS
www.createforless.com
Discount online retailer with a huge selection of beads and jewellery-making equipment, as well as felt, fabric and general craft materials.

HOBBY LOBBY
Visit www.hobbylobby.com for your nearest store.
Crafts retailer stocking a large selection of jewellery supplies, fabrics and general crafts materials.

JO-ANN FABRICS
Visit www.joann.com for your nearest store.
Stocks a wide selection of jewellery, sewing and general craft materials.

KARI ME AWAY
www.karimeaway.com
Novelty buttons and glass beads as well as rickrack in a large variety of colors.

MICHAELS
Visit www.michaels.com for your nearest store.
Large craft supplier stocking an enormous range of craft materials, including beads and jewellery tools, modelling clay, and general art supplies such as paint, glue and glitter.

M&J TRIMMING
www.mjtrim.com
Fancy trims, including rhinestones, crystal beads, sequined flowers, ribbons, lace and beaded braid.

SUNSHINE CRAFTS
www.sunshinecrafts.com
Online retailer stocking a huge selection of craft materials, from beads and jewellery findings, to fabrics and modelling clay.

TINSEL TRADING CO.
1 West 37th Street
New York, NY 10018
212-730-1030
www.tinseltrading.com
Vintage buttons and beads, as well as gorgeous silk and velvet flowers, sequins, metallic tassels, and exquisite ribbons.

index

acknowledgments

Author's acknowledgments

I would like to say a big thank you to Penny Wincer for bringing everything to life with her amazing photography and making this a great project to work on. I would also like to say a huge thank you to Rebecca Woods who has been a fantastic guide for me throughout this book, to Sonya Nathoo for all her brilliant help and support with the design, to Barbara Zuñiga for laying out the book, and to Luis Peral for the lovely styling.

Thank you to all the children who modelled for the book, you have been great! Thanks for your real patience and enthusiasm for all the projects.

A big thank you to my husband Salvatore for all his support and encouragement, my daughter Annaliese for her excitement and enjoyment of being involved in the book, and my mum Wilma for her great support throughout.

Ryland, Peters and Small would like to thank all the children who kindly modelled for this book, including: Amelia, Annaliese, Audrey, Belle, Constance, Dixie-Lillybelle, Edie, Ellis, Elizabeth, Emma, Janae, Julian, Lauren, Lydia, Lily, Mayan and Sean.